Cambridge Young Learners English Tests

Cambridge Movers 4

Examination papers from

University of Cambridge
ESOL Examinations:

English for Speakers of Other Languages

CAMBRIDGE
UNIVERSITY PRESS

CAMBRIDGE UNIVERSITY PRESS
Cambridge, New York, Melbourne, Madrid, Cape Town, Singapore, São Paulo

Cambridge University Press
The Edinburgh Building, Cambridge CB2 2RU, UK

www.cambridge.org
Information on this title: www.cambridge.org/9780521611336

First published 2005
4th printing 2007

Printed in the United Kingdom at the University Press, Cambridge

A catalogue record for this publication is available from the British Library

ISBN-13   978-0-521-61133-6 Student's Book
ISBN-10   0-521-61133-4 Student's Book

ISBN-13   978-0-521-61134-3 Answer booklet
ISBN-10   0-521-61134-2 Answer booklet

ISBN-13   978-0-521-61135-0 Cassette
ISBN-10   0-521-61135-0 Cassette

ISBN-13   978-0-521-61136-7 Audio CD
ISBN-10   0-521-61136-9 Audio CD

Contents

Part 1
– 5 questions –

Listen and draw lines. There is one example.

Paul   Sally   Jill   Jim

Jane   Fred   Daisy

Part 2

– 5 questions –

Listen and write. There is one example.

HOMEWORK BOOK

Homework: .... English ....

1 For which day? ....

2 What to write: ....

3 How long? .... pages ....

4 What about? ....

5 Book to read: 'The .... World'

Part 3
– 5 questions –

What did Jane do last week?

Listen and write the correct day. There is one example.

> Monday, Tuesday, Wednesday, Thursday
> Friday, Saturday, Sunday

Monday

....

....

Part 4
– 5 questions –

Listen and tick (✔) the box. There is one example.

What does Nick want for breakfast?

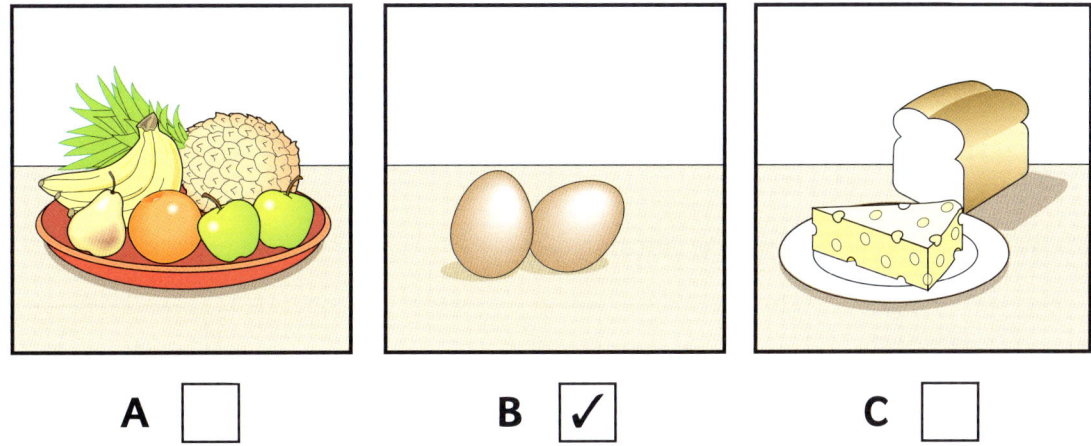

A ☐   B ✔   C ☐

1   Which girl is May's sister?

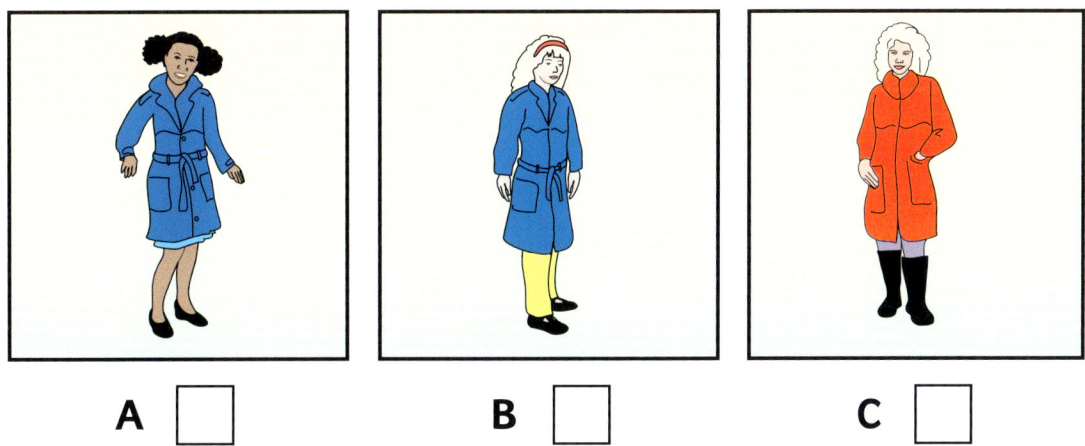

A ☐   B ☐   C ☐

2   Where did Kim play?

A ☐   B ☐   C ☐

7

3 Which animals did Sam like best at the zoo?

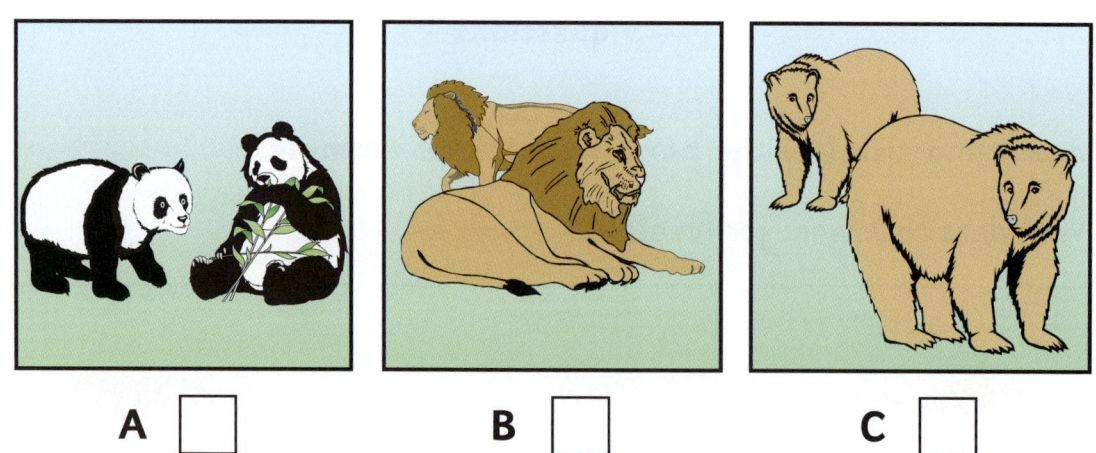

A ☐   B ☐   C ☐

4 What did Jill buy at the shops?

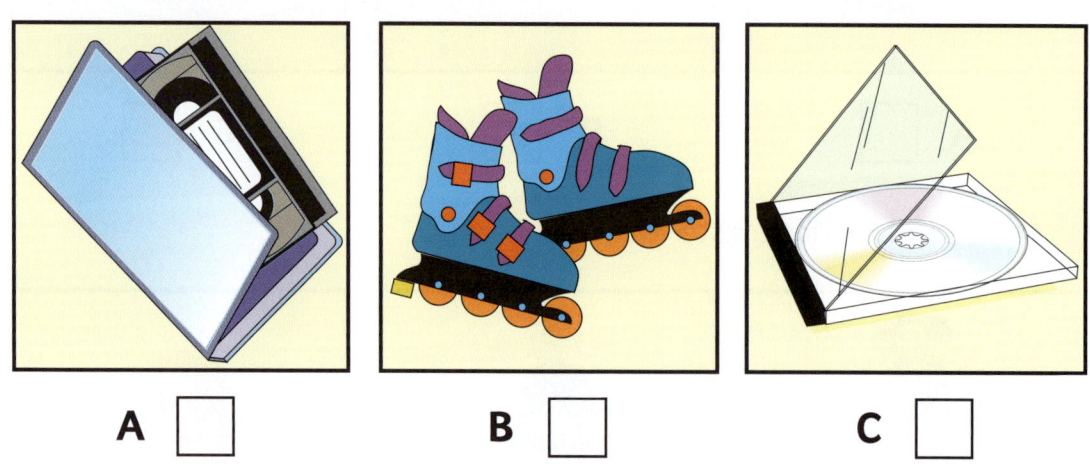

A ☐   B ☐   C ☐

5 What is Ben's Mum cooking for supper?

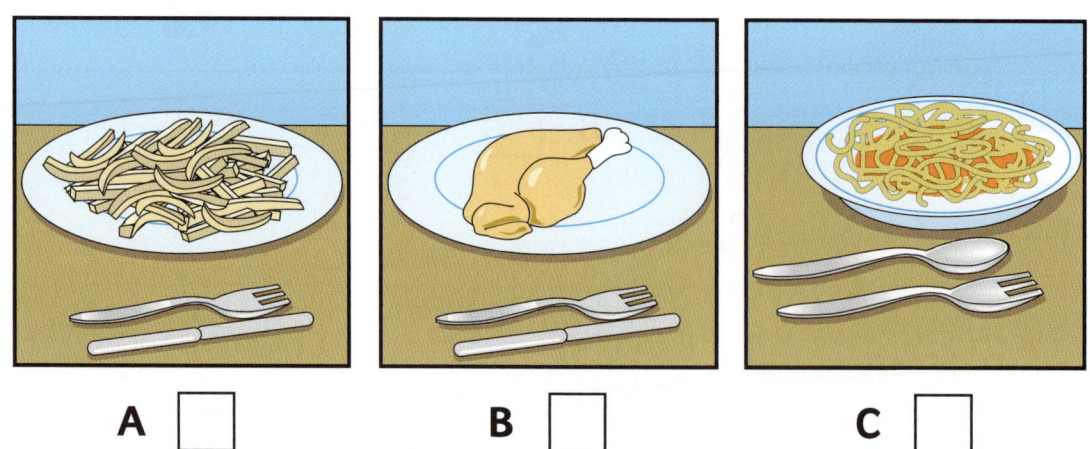

A ☐   B ☐   C ☐

Part 5
– 5 questions –

Listen and colour and draw. There is one example.

Reading and Writing

Part 1
– 6 questions –

Look and read. Choose the correct words and write them on the lines. There is one example.

a balcony

fields

stairs

a road

a forest

doors

a lift

a river

Example

Cars, buses and motorbikes all go on this.   *a road*
....

Questions

1   There are always a lot of trees in this place.
....

2   In a house, for example, you walk up or
down these.
....

3   In the countryside you can often see sheep or
cows in these.
....

4   You open these to go in and out of rooms.
....

5   This often starts in the mountains and goes
down to the sea. Boats can sail on it.
....

6   You can go up to an apartment in this. It is
quick and easy.
....

Part 2
– 6 questions –

Look and read. Write yes or no.

Examples

A parrot is sitting on an old chair.

.... yes ....

There is a toy pirate in the box.

.... no ....

Questions

1   There is a toy lion on its back in front
of some books.
....

2   There is a big spider above the lamp.
....

3   The toy rabbit has only got one eye.
....

4   There is a fan next to some green
bottles.
....

5   The boy is sitting on the floor and
reading a comic.
....

6   There are some skates between the
box and the bag.
....

Part 3

– 6 questions –

Read the text and choose the best answer.

Example

Sue: Hello, Jane. How are you?

Jane: A   I'm going to the market.
      Ⓑ   I'm fine.
      C   I'm John's sister.

Questions

1   **Sue:**   Is this your new dog?

Jane: A   Yes. His name's Ben.
      B   Yes. He was mine.
      C   Yes. He's in a pet shop.

2 **Sue:** Can I give him some of my ice cream?

   Jane: A   No, it isn't!
           B   No, don't do that!
           C   No, he doesn't!

   Sue: All right!

3 **Jane:** Have you got any pets?

   Sue: A   Yes, they are animals.
           B   Yes, tigers in the zoo.
           C   Yes, rabbits. Two black ones.

4 **Sue:** Would you like to come and see them one day?

   Jane: A   Yes, I'd like that.
           B   Yes, you like them.
           C   Yes, they can see them.

5 **Jane:** Can my sister come with me?

   Sue: A   Yes, thanks.
           B   Yes, all right.
           C   Yes, that's correct.

6 **Sue:** Which day do you want to come?

   Jane: A   We can come at the weekend.
           B   We can come on the bus.
           C   We can come for two weeks.

Part 4

– 7 questions –

**Read the story. Look at the pictures and the two examples.
Write one-word answers.**

'Can we sleep in the garden?' said Jill and Sally to their mother one

very ....hot.... evening and she said 'Yes.'

The two girls put blankets on the ....grass.... . They put a

bottle of water and two .... next to the blankets.

They talked quietly, looked at the moon and stars and then they slept.

But at night it was colder than in the afternoon and they woke up. Then

a cat .... off the garden ....

'What was that?' said Jill.

A .... flew above them. 'What was that?' said Sally.

'Jill, are you ....?' said Sally.

'Yes I am, and I'm cold!' said Jill.

Then they picked up the blankets and ....

inside quickly.

In the morning, their mother found them, not outside in the garden, but

inside the house in their beds.

What's the best name for this story?

Tick one box.

An afternoon in the garden ☐

Sleeping under the stars ☐

A picnic at night ☐

Part 5
– 10 questions –

Look at the pictures and read the story. Answer the questions. Do not write more than three words.

David is eleven, and he has two older brothers, Peter and Paul. They like tennis very much. 'Come and have a game with us,' they say to David every day. But David never goes because he doesn't like tennis. He enjoys playing computer games. He plays them all day. His mother often says to him, 'David, don't sit in the house at the computer. Go to the park with your brothers!'

Example

How old is David? .... *eleven* ....

Questions

1   What are the names of David's brothers?

    ....

2   What game do David's brothers enjoy playing?

    ....

3   What kind of games does David like?

    ....

4   Where does David's mother tell him to go?

    ....

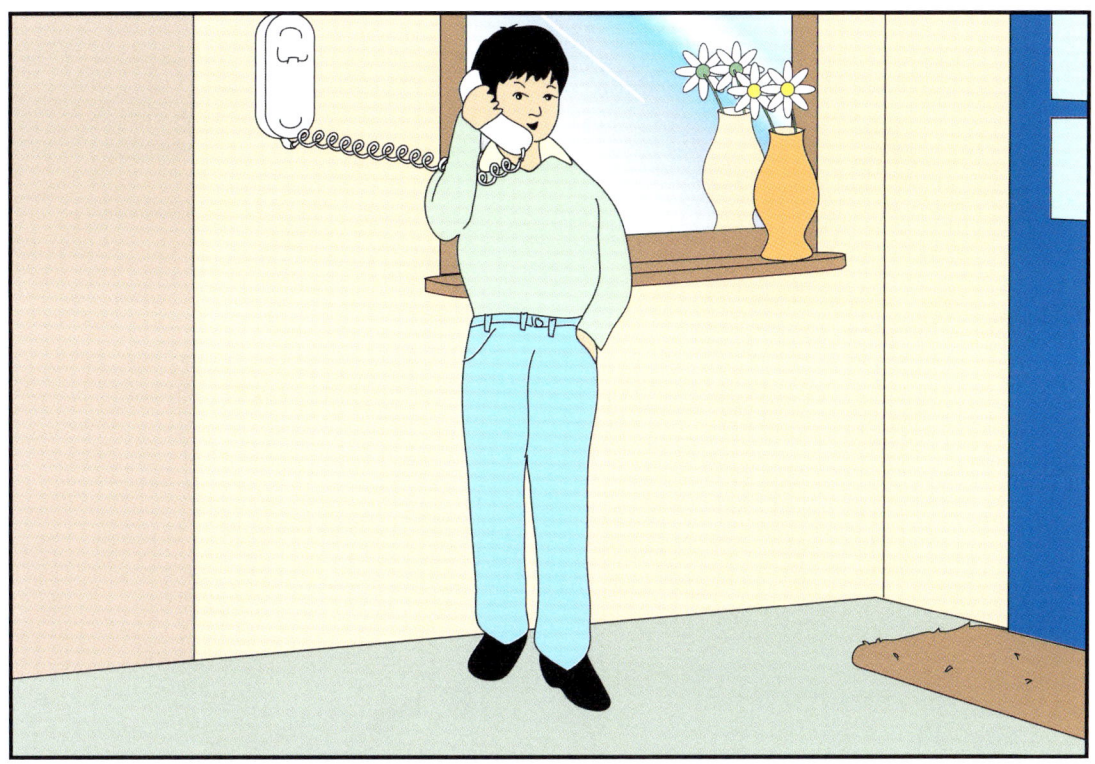

One weekend, David played on his computer all day Saturday, but on Sunday morning he phoned his friend Nick and then went to his house. Nick had a lot of good games in his bedroom. They played there all morning. Then they went to the kitchen and had some cheese sandwiches for lunch, with a drink of orange juice.

5   Which day did David go to Nick's house?   ....

6   Which room did Nick and David play in?   ....

7   What did Nick and David eat for lunch?   ....

On Sunday evening, David's mother said, 'What did you do with Nick? Did you play tennis?' 'Yes,' said David, 'We played after lunch with his two sisters.' 'Oh, that's good, David,' said his mother. 'It was sunny all day!' 'Was it?' said David. 'I didn't go outside.' 'But you did,' said his brothers. 'You played tennis.' 'Ah, but we played tennis inside,' said David. 'We played **table** tennis!'

8   Who played with Nick and David after
     lunch?

     ....

9   What kind of weather did they have
     on Sunday?

     ....

10   What game did David and Nick play?

     ....

Blank Page

Part 6
– 5 questions –

Read the text. Choose the right words and write them on the lines. There is one example.

Pandas

Pandas are beautiful animals and people love

Example   ....them............... . They have white bodies, black legs

and shoulders, black ears and round, black eyes.

The panda's name is sometimes 'panda bear', but is it a bear?

1   .... bears have short legs, big feet, round

2   ears and black noses. Pandas have ....

things, but they are a different kind of animal, some people

3   .... Why? Because they

4   .... eat meat, fish or fruit. Brown, black

and white bears can eat those foods, but pandas can only eat

one kind of plant.

5   There aren't a lot of pandas .... the world

now.

Example	it	him	them
1	Any	Every	All
2	these	that	this
3	says	saying	say
4	don't	didn't	doesn't
5	in	on	at

Listening

Part 1
– 5 questions –

Listen and draw lines. There is one example.

Peter   Jill   Sally   Fred   Daisy   Jim   John

Part 2
– 5 questions –

Listen and write. There is one example.

STAR CITY SWIMMING POOL

Name: .... Emma Carey ....

1   How old: ....

2   Lives in: .... Street

3   Name of swimming
      class: ....

4   Teacher's name: Paul
                   ....

5   Buys: ....

Part 3
– 5 questions –

What did Peter do last week?

Listen and write the correct day. There is one example.

Monday, Tuesday, Wednesday, Thursday
Friday, Saturday, Sunday

....

Monday
....

Part 4
– 5 questions –

Listen and tick (✔) the box. There is one example.

What's the matter with Kim?

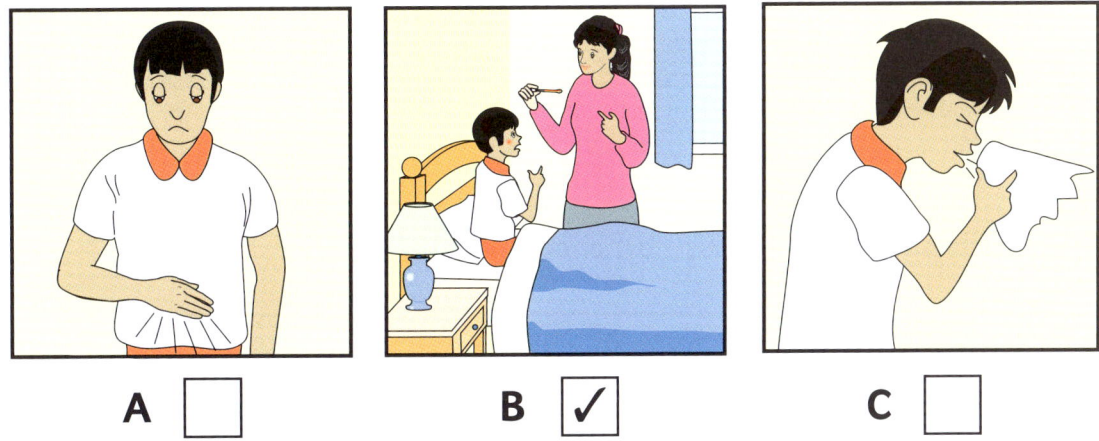

A ☐   B ☑   C ☐

1   What did Jane have for lunch today?

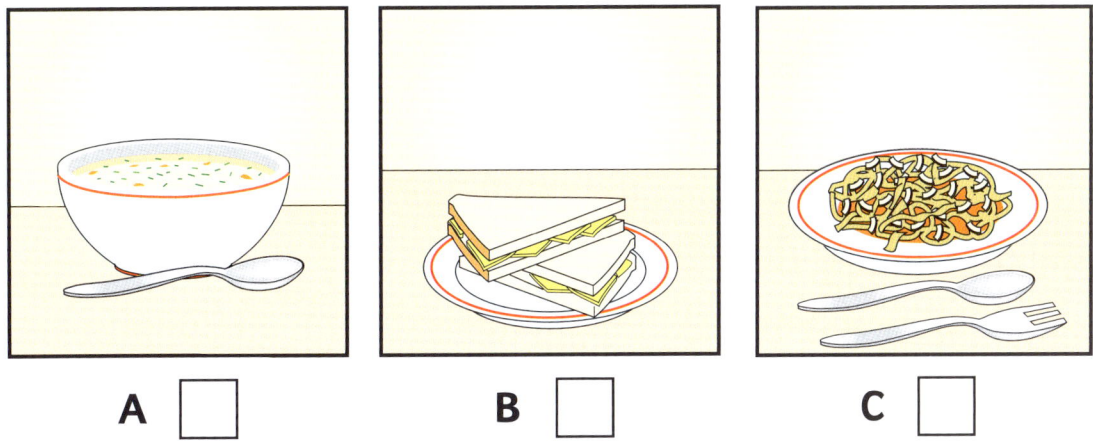

A ☐   B ☐   C ☐

2   Which girl is Ann?

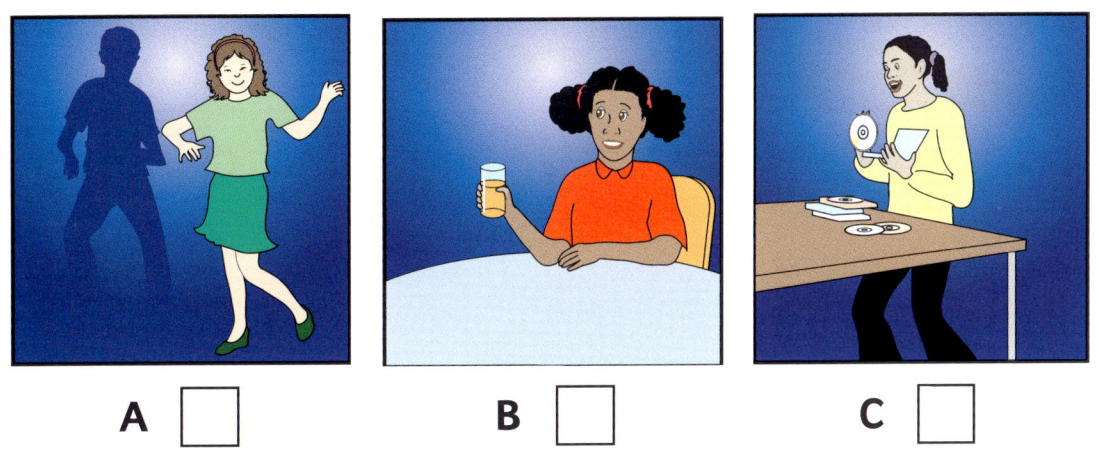

A ☐   B ☐   C ☐

3   What does Mary choose to do?

A   ☐   B   ☐   C   ☐

4   Which photo does Nick's dad choose?

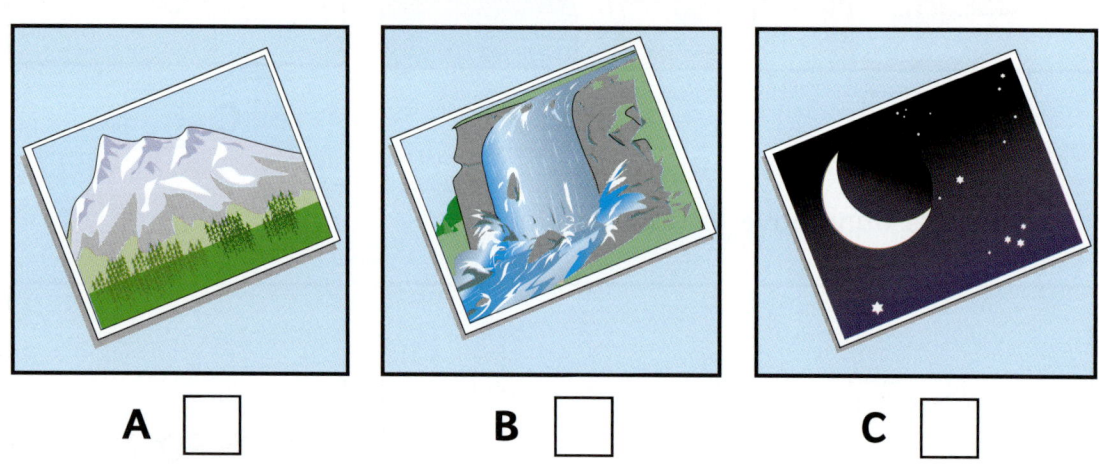

A   ☐   B   ☐   C   ☐

5   How does Sue's mum go to work?

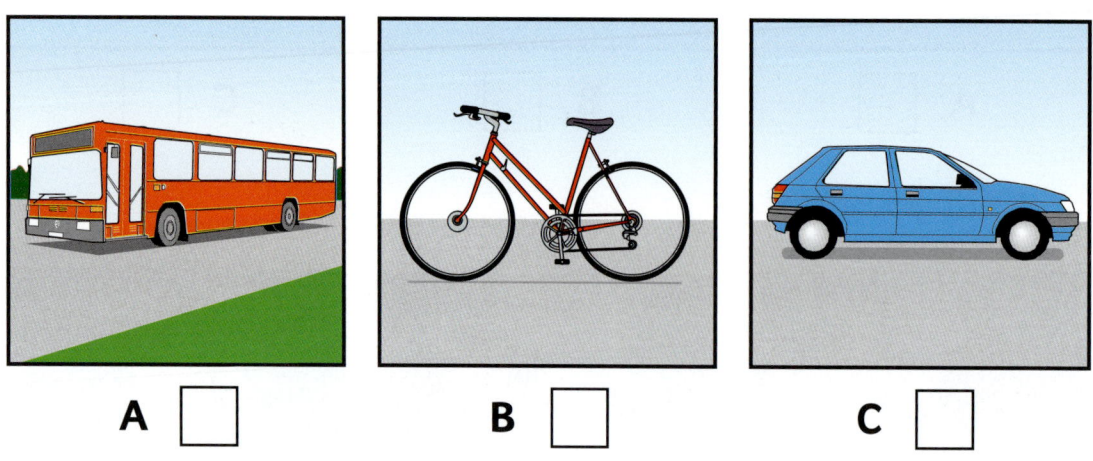

A   ☐   B   ☐   C   ☐

Part 5

– 5 questions –

Listen and colour and draw. There is one example.

Reading and Writing

Part 1

– 6 questions –

Look and read. Choose the correct words and write them on the lines. There is one example.

a supermarket

a park

a shoulder

a market

a zoo

a cinema

a video

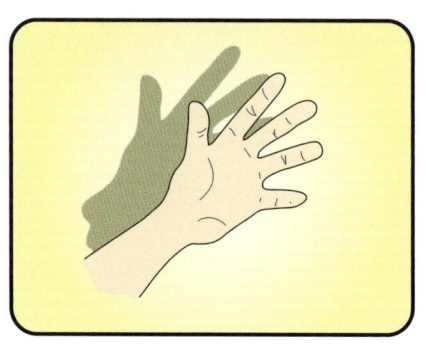

a hand

Example

This is the part of the body at the bottom of
a person's arm.

a hand
....

Questions

1   You can find this green place in a town.
People enjoy sitting, walking or playing
games there.

....

2   People can buy all kinds of food in this shop.

....

3   This is something that people can watch at home.

....

4   This is the part of the body at the top of a
person's arm.

....

5   You can go to this place to see a film.

....

6   Animals like pandas, bears and
kangaroos live here.

....

Part 2
– 6 questions –

Look and read. Write yes or no.

Examples

The boy with black hair is carrying
a rabbit.

.... *yes* ....

There are five children in the pet shop.

.... *no* ....

Questions

1 The white cat is bigger than the
grey cat.

....

2 One of the girls is giving a banana
to the parrot.

....

3 A woman is buying a brown duck.

....

4 The tall man is catching some green
lizards.

....

5 There are more mice than cats in this
shop.

....

6 The boy with red hair is watching
some snakes.

....

Part 3
– 6 questions –

Read the text and choose the best answer.

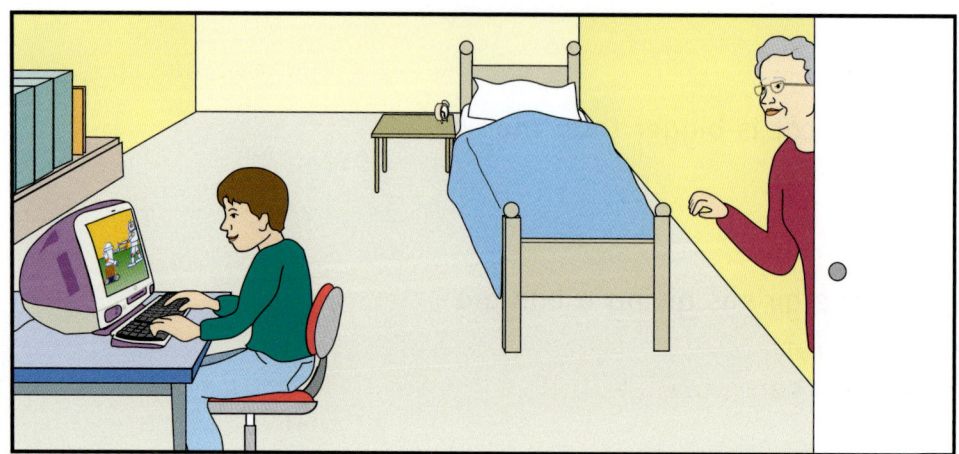

Example

Grandmother: Bill, I've got to take you to your friend's birthday party now.

Bill:
- A Well.
- (B) OK.
- C Then.

Questions

1 **Grandmother:** Where does your friend live?

Bill:
- A Opposite the library.
- B In the river.
- C To the cinema.

2   **Grandmother:** Would you like to go by car?

   Bill:
   A   Yes, I do, thank you.
   B   Oh, yes please.
   C   No, you can walk.

3   **Grandmother:** How many children are coming to the party?

   Bill:
   A   I don't know.
   B   I can't see them.
   C   I haven't got any.

4   **Grandmother:** How old's your friend?

   Bill:
   A   He's fine.
   B   He's eight today.
   C   He's got two brothers.

5   **Grandmother:** Look at that bus! It's very slow!

   Bill:
   A   Yes, it is.
   B   Yes, it can.
   C   Yes, it does.

6   **Grandmother:** Now, which is your friend's house?

   Bill:
   A   Yes, that's one.
   B   Your friend's house is there.
   C   The one with the yellow door.

Part 4
– 7 questions –

Read the story. Look at the pictures and the two examples. Write one-word answers.

My brother, Nick, has a small green frog. His name is Kim.

Kim goes to .... *school* .... every day and all the

children know him. Nick .... *carries* .... him in his

school bag.

Yesterday Kim sat on Nick's desk. He tried to eat Nick's

.... and played with his pencils. In the

lessons Kim .... at the teacher very

carefully. He liked every lesson, but the painting lesson was his favourite. Kim put his two .... in the red

paint and then he .... on Nick's

picture. The teacher saw Nick's picture and she

.... 'This is beautiful!' she said.

Nick was very happy. 'Who's the best frog in the world?' he asked

loudly, and his friends all .... , 'Kim!'

What's the best name for this story?

Tick one box.

Kim's picture ☐

Kim's homework ☐

Kim's school bag ☐

Part 5

– 10 questions –

Look at the pictures and read the story. Answer the questions. Do not write more than three words.

Last weekend my cousin Daisy and I went to our grandparents' house. On Saturday morning we walked to a lake because my grandfather wanted to fish. There are a lot of fish in the lake and he caught ten for supper. My grandmother loves drawing and painting. She sat on the grass and drew some white flowers. She said to us, 'You go sailing. I can watch you.'

Example

Who did the children see last weekend?   their grandparents

Questions

1 Where did they walk to on Saturday morning?   ....

2 How many fish did Grandfather catch?   ....

3 What did Grandmother draw?   ....

We sailed on the lake in Grandfather's small boat. Its name is 'Blue Bird'.
We sailed to a small island and we talked about sharks. Then we saw
something. There was a tall pirate on the island. He saw the boat and said,
'Hello!' very loudly.

4   What is 'Blue Bird'?

     ....

5   Where did the children sail to?

     ....

6   What did they talk about?

     ....

7   Who said, 'Hello'?

     ....

Daisy was afraid. She wanted to go home, but I wanted to see the pirate. He was under a tree. He gave us some fruit, which we ate quickly. After that he showed us his beautiful boat, 'The Red River'. Then we wanted to find some treasure, but the only thing that we found was an old shoe! We threw it in the lake and then we went home.

8   Why did Daisy want to go home?   Because ....

9   What did they eat?   ....

10 What did they find?   ....

Blank Page

Part 6

– 5 questions –

Read the text. Choose the right words and write them on the lines. There is one example.

Football

Example	Football is the favourite sport in ...._a_............ lot of
1	places. To play football you .... the ball
	with your foot. You can hit the ball with your head, but you
2	must not pick .... up.
3	Most young boys and .... girls learn to
4	play football at school, and .... like
	playing football in the playground after school. Children often
5	watch football games with their parents ....
	Saturday or Sunday. People enjoy this sport!

Example	a	an	the
1	kicked	kicks	kick
2	them	it	him
3	every	any	some
4	he	they	she
5	on	in	at

Part 1
– 5 questions –

Listen and draw lines. There is one example.

Jim   Sue   Peter   Pat   Ben   Kim   John

Part 2

– 5 questions –

Listen and write. There is one example.

Park School Library

	Class:	7
1	Name:	Daisy
2	Book:	'My '
3	Video:	
4	CD:	music
5	You can have these for:	One

Part 3

– 5 questions –

What did Bill do last week?

Listen and write the correct day. There is one example.

> Monday, Tuesday, Wednesday, Thursday
> Friday, Saturday, Sunday

Wednesday

....

....

Part 4
– 5 questions –

Listen and tick (✔) the box. There is one example.

What does Nick want?

A ✔   B ☐   C ☐

1   Which animal is Tom's favourite pet?

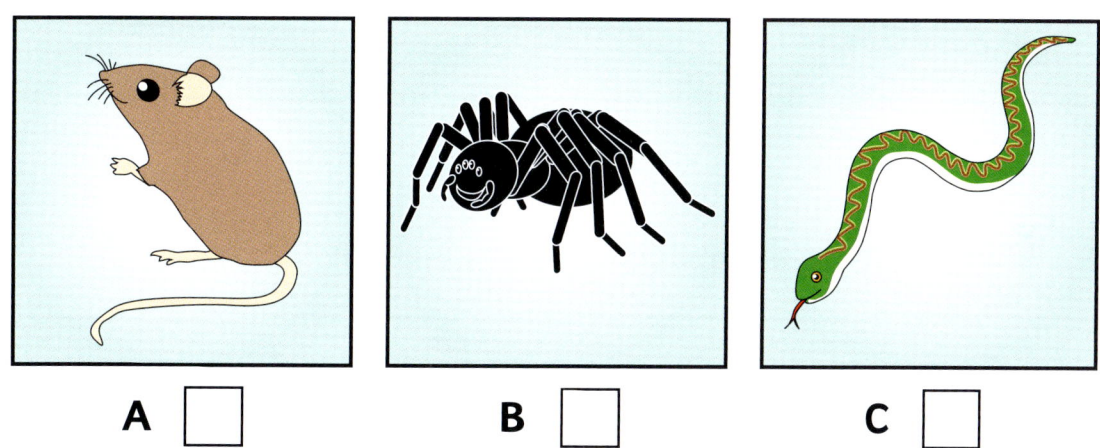

A ☐   B ☐   C ☐

2   Which girl is Fred's cousin?

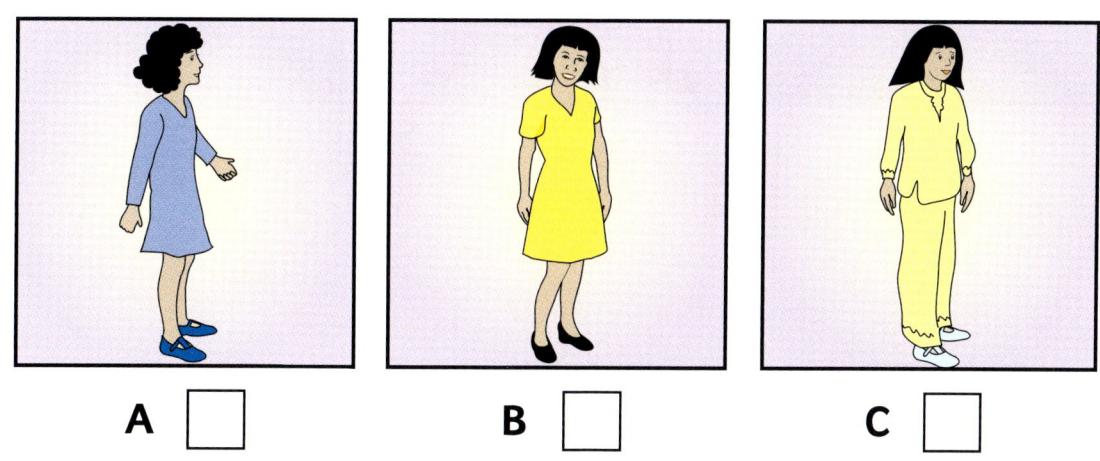

A ☐   B ☐   C ☐

3   What's Kim doing?

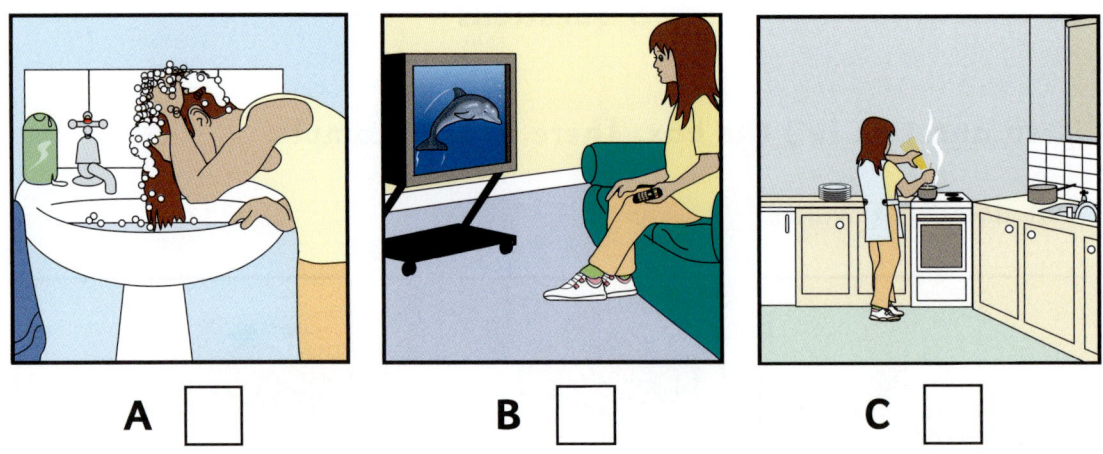

A ☐   B ☐   C ☐

4   What can Paul have for his game?

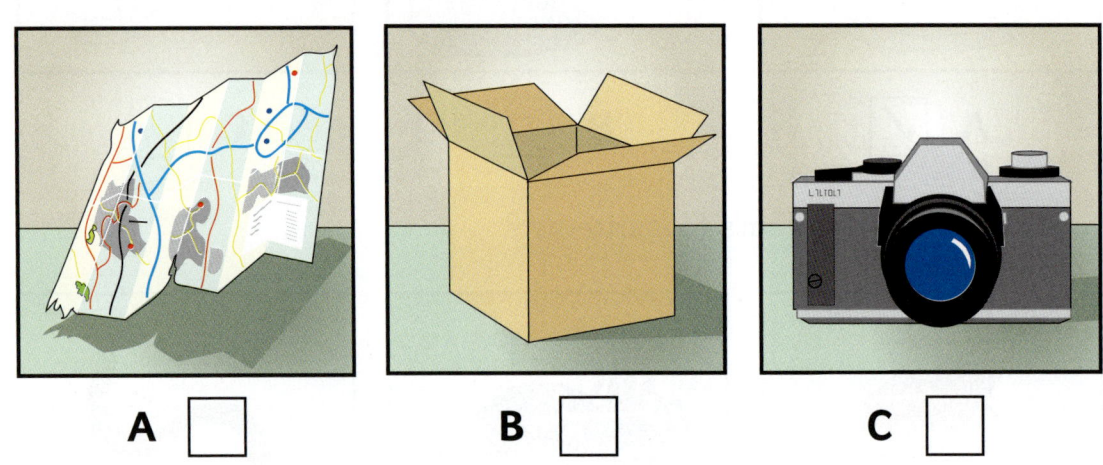

A ☐   B ☐   C ☐

5   What does Sally always do on Monday evening?

A ☐   B ☐   C ☐

Part 5

– 5 questions –

Listen and colour and draw. There is one example.

Reading and Writing

Part 1
– 6 questions –

Look and read. Choose the correct words and write them on the lines. There is one example.

beards

a forest

a bat

plants

a panda

hair

whales

shoulders

Example

People have this on their heads. It can be curly
or straight.

hair
....

Questions

1 This animal flies at night and sleeps in the day.

....

2 You have two of these. They are at the top of
your arms.

....

3 You can find a lot of trees, animals and birds
here.

....

4 Gardens and parks have a lot of these. Some
people put them in their houses.

....

5 Some men have these on their faces below
their mouths.

....

6 These animals live in the sea and are bigger
than sharks.

....

Part 2
– 6 questions –

Look and read. Write yes or no.

Examples

The biggest door is red and green.   yes

There are three children outside the flats.   no

Questions

1   The man who is standing on a balcony is looking at a map.

    ....

2   There are more blue birds than black birds.

    ....

3   The smallest window in the house is square.

    ....

4   The girl on the top floor is wearing a hat.

    ....

5   There is a grey cloud above the mountain.

    ....

6   The man who is washing a window is wet.

    ....

Part 3
– 6 questions –

Read the text and choose the best answer.

Jim is sitting at home after school. He's talking to his mum.

Example

Mum: Hello. Did you have a good day at school?

Jim: A   Yes, I do.
 (B)   Yes, I have.
  C   Yes, I did.

Questions

1 **Mum:** What did you do today?

Jim: A   By bus.
  B   English and music.
  C   With all my friends.

2 **Mum:** Would you like something to drink?

    Jim: A   Yes, I'm thirsty.
              B   Yes, I drank orange juice.
              C   Yes, it's best now.

3 **Mum:** Can you find a glass? They're in the cupboard.

    Jim: A   Yes, there are.
              B   Yes, please.
              C   Yes, OK.

4 **Mum:** Where are you going now?

    Jim: A   To John's house.
              B   At the park.
              C   For basketball.

5 **Mum:** But you've got to do your homework first.

    Jim: A   I haven't got any.
              B   I haven't got one.
              C   I haven't got them.

6 **Mum:** OK, then. You can go.

    Jim: A   I'm fine, Mum.
              B   Yes, you can, Mum.
              C   Thanks. Bye, Mum.

Part 4

– 7 questions –

**Read the story. Look at the pictures and the two examples.
Write one-word answers.**

It was Saturday morning and it was very ....sunny....... .

'Please can I play football in the park with my friends today?' Sally said

to her mother. 'No,' said her mother. Sally started to

.......cry....... . 'On Saturdays we go to see your

grandparents. Now, go and put on your .... ,'

said Sally's mother.

At her grandparents' house, Sally found her grandfather in the garden.

He had a big bag with something .... inside it.

'Come with me,' he said to Sally. They walked down the

.... and came to a field. Grandfather opened

the bag and inside was a ball, some ...., a big

lemon cake and a bottle of orange juice. Sally was very

.... She played football with her grandfather and

after that they sat on the .... and ate the picnic.

What's the best name for this story?

Tick one box.

Sally has a bad day ☐

Sally's picnic in the garden ☐

Sally's game of football ☐

Part 5

– 10 questions –

**Look at the pictures and read the story. Answer the questions.
Do not write more than three words.**

It was Daisy's ninth birthday. Her friends and family gave her a lot of cards and different things. The best thing was the computer which her parents gave her. 'The toys in my bedroom are old,' Daisy said. 'I don't want them now.' She gave them to her mother for her younger sister, Ann. One of the toys was a very old doll with blonde hair and only one eye.

Example

How old was Daisy on her birthday?   *nine*
....

Questions

1   What did her parents give her?
....

2   Why didn't Daisy want her toys?   *Because*
....

3   How many eyes did the doll have?
....

After supper Daisy was very tired and she went to bed. She looked at her bedroom and she was very sad. There weren't any toys in her big red toy box now – only a comic. She tried to read it but she couldn't. She tried to play with the cat but it didn't want to play. She tried to sleep but she was afraid. She wanted her old doll. She got up and went quietly to Ann's bedroom to find it.

4   When did Daisy go to bed?

....

5   What was the one thing in her toy box?

....

6   What did she try and play with?

....

7   Where did Daisy go to find her doll?

....

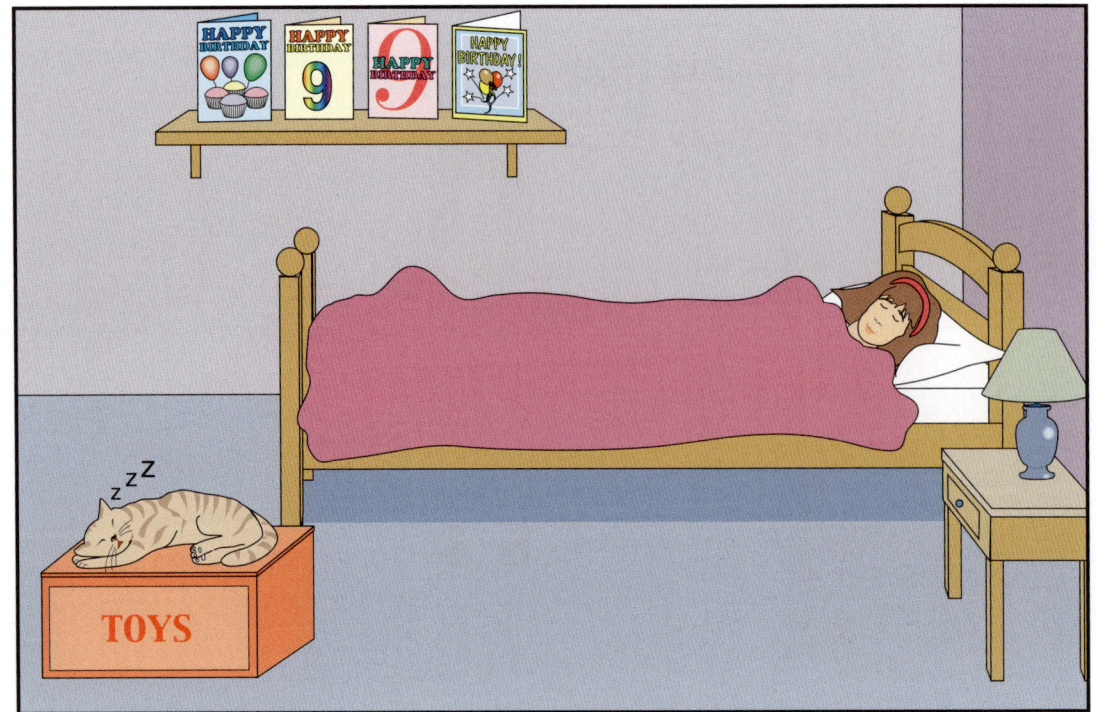

In Ann's room she saw her old doll. It was on the bookcase and she stood on a chair and took it down carefully. Daisy carried the doll to her bedroom and put it in her bed. Then she slept very well. In the morning Ann was sad, but her mum bought her another doll. Then Daisy and Ann were very happy.

8   What did Daisy stand on?   ....

9   Where did Daisy put the doll?   ....

10 Who had a new doll?   ....

Blank Page

Part 6

– 5 questions –

Read the text. Choose the right words and write them on the lines. There is one example.

Cities

There are cities in most countries. Cities are bigger

Example ....than............ towns and villages. There are a lot of

cars, buses, motorbikes and people in them, and

1 .... are not quiet places. It is sometimes

2 difficult to cross the roads and you .... to

be careful. There are a lot of shops and markets. You can buy

3 everything you need .... them. There are

hospitals, banks and libraries. A lot of people

4 .... in the city. In the evening they catch

5 buses and trains .... take them home.

Example	than	or	but
1	that	there	they
2	have	must	can
3	in	on	for
4	work	works	working
5	what	which	who

Blank Page

Find the difference

Story

Find the different ones

Blank Page

Speaking

Find the difference

Story

Find the different ones

Blank Page

Find the difference

Story

Find the different ones